Trials and Tribulations of Being a Redhead

Bullied, Taunted and Teased
for being a Redhead

Nancy K Renner

WestBow
PRESS
A DIVISION OF THOMAS NELSON

ISBN: 978-1-4497-2028-5 (sc)
ISBN: 978-1-4497-2030-8 (e)

Library of Congress Control Number: 2011912204

WestBow Press books may be ordered through booksellers or by contacting:

WestBow Press
A Division of Thomas Nelson
1663 Liberty Drive
Bloomington, IN 47403
www.westbowpress.com
1-(866) 928-1240

Printed in the United States of America

WestBow Press rev. date: 7/27/2011

Introduction

My name is Nancy Renner. In the 1970's, my red hair made me a minority, treated no different than a person of color in an all white community. I was inspired through the spiritual guidance of my church and husband to follow my heart, and, passion for writing; to tell my story. I was bullied, taunted and teased while growing up in a small community because of my red hair. I want to raise awareness of the effects of bullying on children and teens. Most current stories that we hear on bullying is of children and teens fighting back or committing suicide because they can not deal with this form of abuse and harassment. My story is not only about the effects that bullying has had on my life, but, also how I rose above it all. I was bullied from the time I was in kindergarten until I graduated from high school. I went through thirteen years of being bullied. It has taken me thirty years to come to terms with the effects that this has had on my life and write about it. My faith in God and of Jesus Christ as my Savior has given me the courage and wisdom to speak to others on the devastating effects of bullying in schools and elsewhere. If I can help even one person that is being bullied now or someone who has been bullied in the past then I can say that I am fulfilling God's plan that has been laid out before me. *"Trials and Tribulations of Being a Redhead"* are actually memoirs and short stories of events in my life.

Chapters

Growing Up a Redhead
"My Childhood"

I was born Nancy Karlene on September 11, 1962 in a small community hospital in a small town in Ohio. I was born a redhead with blue eyes.

The town, like all the towns in the area, was an all white community, with very few Mexican, and, Amish families. There were no black families in these towns. The black people were all centrally located in the cities; the people growing up in these towns were never really exposed to people of color.

My indifference as a redhead set me apart from all the other kids. I may not have been black, but, I felt the hatred and discrimination amongst all the other kids because of my red hair. I definitely can relate to the same feelings that people of color have gone through in the past. My red hair made me a person of color.

I grew up in the 1960's and 70's before moving out of Ohio in 1980. My family was just a typical poor family with all the financial struggles as everyone else in the community and world at that time. Although, I believe that my family had more money then some of the poorest because the poorest of the poor still had outhouses behind their homes. Back in that day and age, I really did not care who was rich or who was poor. All I knew was the obvious and that was; rich people lived in nicer homes than poor people.

There were no electronics back then, only our imaginations and bicycles. Our first colored television was a used console. The color was off but we didn't care. I also didn't care that the sky was red and the grass was blue, or that the faces were green. It was a colored television and that was all that mattered. Our family was now UP with the Jones. I look back at the "big deal" us kids made when we first got that console television and think "Wow! Kids truly have it made today with colored televisions in nearly every room of the house"

We had a telephone long enough to memorize the number before it was disconnected. When my brothers and I got hungry, we would grab a pan and pour oil in it before popping some popcorn. I loved to see the lid rise on the pan from the force of the popcorn.

My dad was a chicken hauler so we never went hungry. Mom always had plenty of chicken to fry up. On occasion, when there was no chicken to fry up, my Mom would fry up liver, onion and taters. Oh, how I hated liver, but, it was either eat what was fixed for dinner, or, starve. As a family, we always sat at the kitchen table for our meals, together. Nowadays, most families scatter throughout the house or sit in front of a television to eat.

As a child I used to say this simple prayer while sitting at the table with my brothers. ***"God is Great, God is Good, Let us Thank Him for our Food...Amen"*** I loved saying that prayer and I felt terrible if I ate without saying it.

Holidays

Holidays were the best time of the year. Christmas was my favorite. All of us kids may not have gotten everything we wanted, but, we were always surprised by our parents. We would each pull a sock from our dresser and hang it up on the wall to be filled by Santa.

I remember waking up and opening up the front door to see a huge box full of toys and clothes. At first we all thought Santa dropped it off, but, soon we realized that the local church actually dropped off the goods.

I wore a beautiful blouse that I had found in with the gifts. I wore that blouse to school after winter break, BIG MISTAKE! A girl came up to me at school and told me that the blouse I was wearing was hers, and she wanted it back because her parents made her give it to the poor families for the church charity drive against her wishes. I went home took it off and took it back to school so she wouldn't tease me about it. Of course, that didn't stop the teasing because she bragged about how she had to throw it away because I had worn it. Kids were mean and had no compassion.

Thank God, that I had my family. My parents always saw to it, that we had memorable holidays. Especially my Dad! There were some Christmas's when Dad would get us kids all up in the wee hours of the mornings because he couldn't wait any longer to see the expressions on all our faces. Dad anticipated Santa's arrival as much as we all did.

Even when we were all old enough to know the truth about Santa, we couldn't let on because "to receive you must believe".

My Mother

There were no cell phones or Nintendo games. We didn't have microwaves or even an automatic clothes washer and dryer. My mom washed our clothes with a manual ringer washer and hung them out to dry.

My Mother and I may not have always seen eye-to-eye, but, I truly love and appreciate my Mother for all that she has done for me.

No one can ever replace my Mother. She is a very strong woman and I love her dearly. My Mother stayed strong when taking care of my ailing Dad whom I miss and love so much. There is not a day that goes by without missing Dad. I know that my Dad is in Heaven with our Lord Jesus Christ. He is most definitely in a much better place.

Since I was the only girl, I always had my own bedroom, but, all three of my brothers always had to share a bedroom. This of course, left no room for privacy. Not that it mattered much, because we all had curtains for doors.

There was an awful lot of fighting in our house. I remember once when my middle brother started yelling throughout the house about my oldest brother, and, that he was doing something inappropriately. My mom just flew off the handle, rambling and screaming, all the while she was stomping her feet, and, all I could think of was; "God! Please take me away"

Revenge w/ Regrets

Growing up a redhead in a hick town in Ohio was very hard. All the grownups used to say "Nancy, you have the most beautiful red hair". I would think to myself "you've got to be kidding me, I look hideous". I think that I had the lowest self esteem ever, while in school. Kids used to poke fun at me and call me RED.

To this day I hate to be called RED. One girl in particular, from kindergarten through till I graduated from high school, taunted me, poked fun at my hair and teased me on every level. If I saw her today; I would not even acknowledge that I ever knew her.

I got my revenge on this girl back in the early 1980's I was out with the girls and ran into her boyfriend in a local establishment where they were playing live music. He wanted to me to step outside so he could kiss me.

Knowing that he was engaged to "one of the girls who had bullied me all my life", I couldn't help but to jump at the opportunity to GET BACK!

You are thinking how mean, but, I am thinking this is nothing compared to what I went through in school because of this girl and others.

I truly regretted that incident, and, I would never allow myself to ever stoop to that level of stupidity, again. I was no better than the bullies throughout my life. It was wrong and I knew it, but couldn't resist.

Elementary Bullying

Being bullied in elementary school wasn't as bad as being bullied in junior high and high school. I used to go home feeling sick to my stomach and I would always have a pounding headache.

Kids would tease and elbow me in the ribs, all the while calling me RED. I actually on occasion tried to buy friendship with candy and gum. This worked! For awhile, okay! Maybe for a few hours, but, it was enough time for me to feel some form of relief.

There were many times when I didn't understand an assignment, rather than raise my hand and ask a question; I just didn't ask the question for fear of being ridiculed.

In the past if I asked a question in the classroom, someone would speak out and say "Teacher! RED has a question" "because she is stupid" under their breath. Then you could hear them all snickering and as I would turn around, I would get a glimpse of their eyes rolling.

Kids would crowd me out of the lunch line because "Redheads didn't need to eat. Eating will only put more spots on their white skin".

Then there was the time when another little girl threw gum in my hair. I remember the girl laughed and said "the fire in your hair will melt it out" I pulled my hair; actually, I broke all the strands that surrounded the gum. I wanted to cry, but, I held it all in. Like, I had to do many times before.

I hated school so bad because of how mean the kids were that I didn't care if I ever learned anything. I stopped asking questions, I stopped raising my hand and I became very withdrawn in elementary school.

I was labeled as "SHY" by the teachers. Parents! If you have an outgoing child and he or she becomes withdrawn in school or at home; take this as a sign. Ask questions and talk to the teachers and principal.

I was visiting my mother the other day and she said she had something for me. She handed me some of my old grade cards from school and as I was reviewing them, it hit me like a ton of bricks.

My God! I missed a lot of school back then. One grade card for my second grade shows that I missed forty-two days total for the year.

My third grade, grade card shows I missed thirty five days out of that year. My fourth grade, grade card I missed forty days. Get the picture? These kids made me feel so inferior and frightened that I did not want to go to school.

Growing up I had sinus headaches that weren't as bad as I pretended them to be. My sinus headaches always served their purpose for an excuse to not go to school.

I remember complaining to my mom about the bullying, and, all she would say to me was "Nancy, just ignore them". Yeah, like that was going to work. And NO it didn't work. It was as though the more I ignored them the worse the bullying got to be towards me.

No one understood the pain and anguish I was going through. This bullying affected every aspect of my learning capabilities. I lagged behind most all the students. I felt as though every time I spoke up someone taunted me. It got to the point where I just didn't speak up and ask any questions, PERIOD!

I remember playing on the playground and feeling so alienated watching all the other kids laugh and play games with one another.

I do, however, remember being invited to one of the girls in my class's birthday party when I was seven years old. She was one of very few kids who treated me nice, her name was Deb. I enjoyed myself and I remember feeling like I belonged. That was very, very, short lived, though.

Out of all the boys in grade school, there was only one that treated me nicely and his name was David Kallison. We could talk about anything and he was very polite to me. He was my friend and then he moved away. That was the way it went for me! Dag Nabit! He was the only REAL friend I had in grade school. He always talked to me and those talks made me feel good.

Being a Minority

I was categorized and treated with the same racism as a minority was treated back in the 1970's. Now, I am not saying that to be mean or in a racist tone. It is just that there were so few redheads and so few Mexican and Amish families that we were treated together as a minority group. My parents were good friends with most all the Amish and Mexican families in the area. I felt very close to them as though they were a part of my family. Kids in school used to call the Mexicans "tomato pickers", "spicks" and "wetbacks". It was because they were different that the kids in the area were mean to them. I think that is because maybe their parents felt the same way. I used to pray to God at night to bless our town with some black families so as to take the heat off of the Mexicans, Amish and myself.

I was never racist and I loved people of color and indifference. I had my Dad's "Heart of Gold"

"Dad loved to help whoever needed him. He always made himself available and never turned anyone away. Dad and I traveled the countryside together. We have taken many road trips across the United States and we discovered many new roads that were not even in the road atlas, YET! We always had enjoyed each others company. No one can take those memories away".

Junior High/ High School days - 1979

High School Days

There were only a couple of redheads in the entire school. By the time I entered junior high there were two redhead girls and one redhead boy in our grade.

Junior high school was tough, I was always the last to get picked for any type of sports and when all the girls would gather together to talk about boys, I was always left out of the conversation.

I knew I did not have a chance at ever being kissed by a boy because I felt that I was this very ugly creature with my red hair and white speckled skin. The girl that always took pleasure in bullying me even told me so, "Nancy! No boy is ever going to like you because your hair is on fire and you are a spotted leopard"

This girl was a popular tomboy in school, but, had a lot of friends that followed her mean ways. She was a bully and I learned to despise her throughout the years.

During my junior high and high school days, I was thrown up against lockers, elbowed in the ribs, socked in the stomach, threatened and dragged out of school by my red hair.

I was sitting in Home Economics class, when a girl, who was fairly new and always looking for acceptance; decided to join the bandwagon of bullying me by going one step further. She started whispering to me and when I wouldn't turn my head to acknowledge her, she started getting louder. She said "Red, why you ignoring me?" "You think you are better than me?" "Answer me when I talk to you" "I'm gonna throw you out like the trashy redhead that you are"

I finally looked at her after all the taunting to say "What did I ever do to you?" But, as soon as I looked her way, she jumped up out of her seat and started yelling "What are you looking at me for?" then she grabbed my hair.

She was pulling and I was hanging on to prevent my hair from being pulled from my scalp all the while she was dragging me down the hallway and on outside of the building.

She slammed my head up against the wall and I remember seeing stars. At that time, two Mexican sisters pulled her away and started slamming her up against the wall. It wasn't until the sisters stepped in that the teachers decided to break it up.

I was suspended from school for the incident. My Mom asked me what I did to be suspended and I said "NOTHING" And, she said; Well nobody does "nothing" and gets suspended! You're grounded!'

I always wondered why that girl hated me so badly. Was causing injury to someone really worth her desire to fit in?

Of course, I knew the answer to that question. Yes! Kids can be so misguided. This new girl wanted to be accepted by all the other kids in our school. Picking on "the redhead" gained her the acceptance she was longing for. How pathetic for kids to think that any good can come out of inflicting pain onto others. And, where were the adults?

There was never any form of intervention by an authority figure between the bullies and myself. What I went through on a day-to-day basis had to be dealt with by me, alone. People turn a blind eye and deaf ear to the ridicule of redheads. It just becomes accepted by society, but, this accepted behavior is a form of ignorance and it hurts.

Railroad Walk Retreat

Retreating to the Tracks

A way for me to forget was to retreat to hiking the railroad tracks. After being bullied all day at school, a nice walk on the tracks was the counseling I needed. It was a way for me to let my emotions go.

I loved those walks. To see nature at its glory was riveting. It's hard to explain the greatness in those walks. It is truly remarkable to smell the fresh air, to see the deer run, and to watch the rabbits and their babies play in fields.

I would look up and see a huge bird circling those baby rabbits and think to myself, "even animals become victims, they get attacked, die and then eaten, at least I am still alive"

It was also very daring to see a train speed by and feel the wind from the railroad cars whisk by and hit my face. Once in a while I would place a penny on the rail; after the train went by I would pick up the flattened penny and put it in my pocket for good luck.

Unfortunately today it is illegal to take a walk on the tracks. How sad! At least I have those memories to cherish forever.

No matter where I retreat to escape the pain, I still have to face reality.

Reality is what it is and then some.

My Brothers

While in high school I did a lot of babysitting for my family. I would watch my brothers all the time and I look back at how I treated them and it makes me feel just horrible.

I was so tormented at school, that when I came home I took my anger out on the only ones who I felt I was not inferior to, "MY BROTHERS".

One of my brothers used to wet the bed so I would use that problem as a way to get back at him when he misbehaved. I used to call him "pee pants", he would cry and run off and leave me alone.

Little did my brothers know that I was so bullied at school that any little teasing that they may have suffered, was nothing to what I went through on a day to day basis. But, by calling my brother a name, I was no better than the kids were at school to me.

Stereotyping Redheads

Growing up, I was always told "you gotta watch out for them Redheads because they're hot tempered" Well Redheads ARE hot tempered "because" of all the taunting received while growing up. Redheads have always been stereotyped as hotheaded or fire tempered. Prolonged harassment is cause for anyone to lash out.

Church

Church, on the hand, was no different than the experiences I had in school. I felt, not only the kid's eyes and teasing tongues, but, the adults too.

I loved learning the gospel, but, how could people be so mean in such a holy place. Parents would gather after church for a picnic with the entire congregation.

One parent in particular came up to tell me that I needed to go home. I never wanted to go back to church. Every time I thought of church, I began to think of how those people treated me.

One lady even came to me when I was around thirteen years old and said to me "Don't you think your mother should be here too, with her children, instead of just dropping you all off?" She just looked at me and then rolled her eyes and turned to the others and laughed while shaking her head.

How was I to answer her or why would I even want too? I hated church but I loved God.

I secretly wanted to be a part of a Church and the congregation. For me to witness others smiling and bonding with one another at church was just a dream for me. One of which, I was never a part of, but, longed to be.

My Teen Years / 1979

When I turned sixteen my life literally started to change. I started to develop and mature. I had begun to develop a nice slender body. BUT, I still had the red hair, freckles and white legs.

Oh! To be one of those girls with tan legs. I could only dream! It felt really strange to me when boys from nearby towns would cruise through our hick town and whistle at me.

These boys would drive by me while walking, and yell out of their car "hey cutie, what's your name?" or "HEY! Want to go partying" For me that was unreal. Boys, being interested in me, a REDHEAD. No way!

It was really hard to get used to kids, boys and people in general; from outside our small community, being nice to me.

A beautician where I went to get my hair cut (the Farrah Fawcett doo) told me that I had the most beautiful red hair. Normally I would say yea right, but, this time I went home and just stared at myself in the mirror. I actually saw the prettiness in myself.

This is what all the outsiders cruising through our town saw in me too, A beautiful redhead. *Although, I could see what some adults saw in me, I still felt inferior to others.*

Senior Picture

Senior, Pregnant AND Graduation

By my senior year in high school, my self-esteem was so low that any attention I received from outsiders of the community was a blessing to me. I thrived on that attention.

I was very naïve and had no idea on what having a boyfriend was like or what a relationship entailed. I just took the attention and ran with it. Up until my senior year, I had normal crushes on boys; after all, I was a girl. But, I never had a serious boyfriend, especially, a boyfriend from our community.

The boys that I went to school with were immature and saw me as "that Redhead" and I didn't want to be caught dead with any boy from my school. Besides, boys were after only one thing and it wasn't "friendship". I was a virgin and I was proud of it"

Actually I didn't even know what the word "virgin" meant. I just knew that I was untouched and that was fine by me.

One particular boy from a different town kept pursuing me and I didn't know how to react to his persistence. I think I was more flattered than anything.

He told me that I was very pretty and that if anything ever happened to me, he would always be there to take care of me because, in his own words "I am from a large family of devout Catholics and you'll never have to worry about anything" This conversation pertained to sex. I was scared and I didn't want to go that far.

He picked me up one night and took me to a party where there was alcohol. I felt compelled to fit in, so I drank with him. He had his way with me and I believed him. I was stupid! And, I became pregnant. Of course, he wanted nothing more to do with me after I told him I was pregnant.

Telling my parents was a very hard thing for me to do. I would rather have been dragged out of the school and beat up repeatedly than tell my parents.

I made the decision to tell my mom first. Her response was "How could you be pregnant? You've never even had a boyfriend" I was thinking, "Well, Okay, You're right! So, now what?" I begged mom to tell dad because I didn't have the courage to break his heart.

My Dad was very forgiving. I realized then that my dad had an unconditional love for me that I never saw before. Dad just looked at me and said "Well, I guess you're gonna have a baby, we'll get through this" Dad never yelled or looked down on me. My father and I became very close during this time of my life.

Our family didn't have much money, so, while pregnant I had only three pairs of maternity pants to wear to school. Every three days I would wash my clothes by hand and hang them on the clothes line to dry. I never complained. I didn't mind because I always felt that everything would be okay.

Dad had just suffered his first heart attack and was released from the hospital when I went into labor. I gave birth to a little girl and named her Amy. Amy was my first born and God blessed me to have this bundle of joy on Dad's birthday, July 1, 1980.

This event in my life would prove to be very challenging. A single mother determined to leave the town and all the bullies behind. I had a long road ahead of me, but, I would prevail.

To be a pregnant senior in high school, worst of all, the very place where I was taunted, teased and bullied all my life, was not going to be easy. All I could do, was what I had done most all my life and that was; to hold my head up and ignore all the rest.

I figured that if I was brave enough and had the courage to put up with all of this torment; one more year (my last year of school) would be well worth it to get my diploma and no one was going to prevent me from doing just that.

While pregnant, there was an assignment in Government class or was it Civics, not sure but I do remember the assignment.

All the students in the class kept looking at me while they chose the topic for a research paper. We had to choose this topic from a list that the teacher had. Of course, I was the last person allowed to choose a topic; therefore, there was no choice of the matter. I received the last topic and this topic was on "abortion".

All the students including the teacher, laughed. I smiled and responded with a shrugging of the shoulders.

A few month's later, I walked down the aisle at graduation, and thank God gowns were made big. This excess material accommodated my baby growing inside of me.

At eight months pregnant, in a hot gymnasium in June 1980, I walked down the aisle to receive my diploma. I felt all eyes on me. I held my head up as I was accustomed to doing. I didn't care what anyone thought. I would never see these people again.

No More Bullying

After high school I made it a point to move out of Ohio and as far away from the life that I had lived away from bullying. I moved to Indiana and made friends with people that knew nothing about what I had gone through growing up.

I kept this secret away from my children and friends because, to talk about it, brought up to many unwanted feelings. I made it a special point to NEVER allow anyone to ever bully me again, and, in doing so I became a bully.

If someone even looked at me the wrong way I stood up to that person and if it meant getting physical, WELL! Than so be it! No one was ever going to put me through what I had already gone through. That part of my life was behind me. Or was it?

Realization

It wasn't until years after I graduated that I realized how pathetic these girls really were. I have a very compassionate soul and no matter how bad I was being treated, I always held my head up high.

To be honest, I truly did not know at the time where all that strength was coming from. I just knew that I had a very strong will to survive and a lot of strength from deep inside.

This inner strength allowed me to not fall apart and to always keep my head up, stand tall, and, move forward.

My whole experience in school, growing up molded me into a person I am very proud of being today. I hate violence and bullying! I learned to stand on my own two feet and defend myself against those who tried to belittle me or threaten me in any way.

"Life is like a maze...There is only ONE true path...All of the other paths lead to nowhere...It is not until we find that Right path.... That which will lead us to Jesus and to succeed...In all that God has given and all his blessings in tow" Nancy Renner

Of course, I didn't just change overnight. It took years of a different kind of abuse to make me strong, but, the damage of all the abuse I went through in school made me more vulnerable in an area I had the hardest time at. That area was in relationships with the opposite sex. The old feelings and emotions that I struggled with while in school kept popping up whenever there was any form of conflict within my relationships. Rather than deal with those feelings, I would just get out of the relationship.

I hate conflict. It eats you up inside which is why I try my best to avoid it.

It was because of my experience with the betrayal of the only boy who I trusted and then was betrayed by; that to trust another man was going to prove to be an obstacle in my life. Together, with my lack of trust in others; (because of the bullying) made all relationships difficult.

It took me some time to sit back and re-evaluate myself in order to get the courage up to stand on my own two feet and do what was best for me.

I struggled through two abusive relationships before I realized what was wrong. It was as though I was back in school all over again accepting the abuse; like it was apart of whom I was, AND, the fact that I was missing "Our Lord Jesus Christ" in my life was beginning to take its toll on my mental well-being.

I took the abuse in relationships like I took it in school. Just held my head up high and tried to ignore it. But, there comes a time in your life when you just can no longer ignore abuse.

I had made up my mind to stand my ground. I had also made the decision to seek out a Church to call my own and belong.

Ignoring my past like it never happened was nearly impossible and it was wrong of me to think that I could.

I shouldn't forget because I can not do that (as much as I try) but, I can forgive. By not forgiving, I was missing out on "Our Lord Jesus Christ" and the possibility of ever truly being happy. I needed to open my heart, accept the past memories, move on and forgive.

It wasn't until around my 42nd birthday that I realized that I was never going to be happy unless I let it all go and open up my heart. I did just that! I followed my heart and I found my husband.

He was the man I was destined to be with. He loves my red HAIR! And, He loves God as much as I.

I was missing a proper worshipping place (Church), God, and; our Lord Jesus Christ in my life, and, it was driving me crazy.

I believe that my love for God got me through all the hardships in my life, but, I never fully accepted Jesus Christ as my Savior. My parents christened my brothers and me as babies, but, that was not the same. I say that because I did not understand as a child the importance of being forgiven. Nor did I understand that I needed to personally ask for this forgiveness.

Thinking back I believe God was my inner strength. I know that for whatever reason I had to stray down all the different paths that I chose, God wanted me to raise above all the others.

Out of all the paths there is only one TRUE path. You have to find it, reach out for it and follow it. In doing so, help others to find their TRUE path.

My Prayers

I always prayed on a regular basis.

As a little girl I would kneel down before bedtime every night. As a teenager it varied. I would either kneel or lie in bed, on my back and place my hands up by my mouth to pray.

This is the prayer I said every night as a little girl

"Now I lay me down to sleep
I Pray the Lord my soul to keep
If I should die before I wake
I Pray the Lord my soul to take"

What Had I Done?

My husband and I went out one evening for dinner, when I ran into a lady that I hadn't seen in years. She said "Do you remember me?" And I told her "yes, but vaguely"

She told me something that made me cry and reflect on the person that I had become after graduation. She said that I made such a negative impact on her life and that she had to receive counseling to get through her ordeal.

I felt terrible, as I listened to her talk about how mean I was to her. She reminded me of how I felt in school and all the torment I had endured.

Years ago, I was out with some of my friends and she happened to be in the restroom where I pushed her up against a wall and yelled at her, scaring her half to death.

This incident made her fear for her life and therefore became very withdrawn. I intimidated her and I bullied her to the point that she never came around again.

The realization of my attitude most definitely had to change. I made it a point when I moved out of Ohio that I would never be bullied again and that I would stand up to anyone that made me feel threatened.

Sure, I needed to stand up for what was right, but in doing so; I could not continue to do onto others for which they have done unto me. "Others" were not the bullies in school because I no longer lived there or surrounded myself with their hatred. I had to forgive and show more compassion. The entire human population was not the people of the community in which I was raised.

There is a whole world of nice people and I needed to open my eyes and see that. This lady did just that for me, she made me see the impact of all the bullying I received growing up and the role that it played in my life.

What had become clear to me is that I had not let my past go completely, and, those thirteen years of abuse is a lot for one person. I may be strong, but, others going through this may not be as fortunate. It had become obvious to me that I needed spiritual guidance.

"The emptiness inside that I felt was of missing Jesus Christ…I just couldn't see that this was reason for my un-gratification and even though I prayed I believe that I missed the glory of belonging to a Church and of being a part of the bigger picture. I have wanted this all my life but I let my past influence my involvement"

Spiritual Guidance

My husband and I discussed the importance of going to Church and getting involved with the community of the congregation, but, the decision of which Church to attend was always an issue and I believe that it stems back to my childhood days.

We talked for years about which church to go to, but, just never could find THE one. I guess in the back of my mind I was still fighting those memories of my childhood days and my experiences with church.

I think I was actually scared. Crazy I know! I just could not forget all of my past bad experiences. It wasn't until recently after my Dad passed away that I saw what my parents saw in a local church that they attended.

The church and the congregation were just wonderful people. When I met them I felt like I was where I needed to be and it was a magnificent feeling.

I now know why my Dad wanted me to attend with him so badly. If I could go back into time, I would, but I can't.

My Mom is still here with us and I am making it a point to join with her in attending church regularly. I am not going to let my past influence my decision to not attend church ever again.

My husband and I were baptized on April 6, 2011 and we joined The Pleasant Lake Mennonite Church on May 1, 2011. Thank you God, for giving me the strength, to open my eyes and see the light. Actually, it was the pastor of the church that said to me "We all have a talent within each and every one of us; our talents allow us to share and give back to the community and the church". It was after our talk that I decided to start writing and see where it leads me.

Passion in Writing for Awareness in Bullying

I may not be a professional writer, but, I feel compelled to get this out, in my own words. No editing, just me and my story. I want to bring about awareness to something that I never liked to discuss before because of all the harsh feelings that I have harbored over the years.

For all the children (especially redheads) out there in the world today I would tell them to just be true to themselves.

Okay!

So to tell a child that is like telling a child who is being bullied to suck it up and just ignore the others. Alright forget that! Report bullying to someone such as a principal, teacher or guidance counselor in order to raise an awareness to what is happening. Bullying hurts and it damages persons self esteem. I know, because I have been hurt by it.

According to the "Wikipedia" website; red hair is the rarest natural color in humans.

Some myths about red hair are that the color will soon die out in the future. Red hair has been around since the creation of man and woman and will unlikely disappear any time soon. COME ON PEOPLE!

After doing some of my own research to determine if I was the only one (at the time I always felt alone), who was tormented because of my red hair; I found that there is a history of modern-day discrimination of redheads.

In Britain, there is a name for prejudice against redheads and it is called "gingerism". Gingerism is compared to "racism". There have been reported cases in the United Kingdom of racism, and hate crimes against redheads, but, the UK disputes those claims.

In America, some bullies are portrayed in movies and television shows as having red hair. How IRONIC!

When I see a picture portraying Mary Magdalene with red hair, I feel good inside because I know that Jesus loved Mary Magdalene, no matter her hair color.

So, was it just me or were there others that were harassed and bullied because of having red hair? Did we all (redheads) just keep quiet and tolerate the bullying and teasing? Maybe I will get a positive response from my writings. Maybe I won't! Getting the word out that bullying redheads or any other person for that matter is wrong. As a parent, or other "authoritive figure", we need to put more pressure on the schools for a "zero tolerance" on harassment, taunting and bullying of any kind towards any person.

As a victim of bullying, I can fully understand and relate to others on the profound impact that this subject has had on every level of my life. I have kept this secret for thirty years, and, I have finally found the courage to speak and write about how bullying has affected me.

Most children and teens would not have the ability to cope as I have had. How many of our young ones lives have we lost due to suicide? How many have run away from home? Some children and teens may not have coped with the abuse as I have.

I have become aware of a new type of torture on redheads and that is of the cartoon "South Park" making jabs by calling redheads "Ginger". This is wrong and I believe the creators know that it is wrong. If the creators did their homework on the subject of poking fun at redheads, they would have known that this was racism and a form of discrimination.

These past couple of years I have noticed that many of Hollywood's stars were changing their hair color to red.....Really? I have also noticed that many teens are dyeing their hair black and putting bold red stripes in their hair. That was unheard of years ago. I wished this would have happened much sooner. Maybe I would not have had to go through such torment as a young teen like I did, if redheads were more popular in the public eye.

Or maybe it was just the school I attended and the closed minded kids I was raised with and went to school with. If only they had a clue on how bad they had made me feel growing up. Not that they would care any!

I do hope though, that each and every kid that teased me in school has a redhead child or grandchild. I guess this would be a blessing for me to see this happen to them. Will they continue to tease their own flesh and blood? Probably not, because they had no clue how damaging their teasing was to me and others.

How would everyone feel if they were being poked fun at because of something as normal as "hair color" or the shape of the nose, amount of body fat, pimple, freckles, or anything else that distinguishes a teenager from the grown population.

Many grownups do know what its like to be bullied. So we adults need to put a stop to bullying and not tolerate it anywhere, especially, in the schools.

Airing all of this out feels so good. Never again will I allow for anyone to bully me again. If I write about just some of my experiences and get the word out, maybe I can help someone else. Now, that would be a blessing!

Outside of Bullying

Outside of school and the bullying, I had fun growing up. I retreated to long walks on the railroad tracks with my brothers, aunts and uncles. They were family and never bullied or teased me because of my hair color.

I also took long bike rides with my family and a couple of friends that also never teased me. My brothers and I used to make cardboard box club houses out of discarded refrigerator boxes. Those were the days that I wish to never forget.

I have always felt that if you want to do something...Do it! Don't let anyone hold you back from following your dreams. Throughout all that bullying, I was going to persevere. I made it a point to do just that. Don't get me wrong, abuse from bullying stays with you. But, you don't have to let it control your life and allow those bad actions of others bring you down to the point where you are made to feel worthless. This is what the bullies want and by becoming withdrawn, they win.

The bullies in my life may have won the first round because I did become withdrawn in school and my self-esteem was at its all time low, but, I defeated them in the end. I raised above all their abuse.

The best way to take some control of your emotions is to shield yourself from deep within and always pray to God. Ask God for strength, encouragement, endurance and bravery. Always bounce back and hold your head up high. It may seem impossible at times, so tell yourself...I can! I can!.. *Pity is a terrible thing to waste on yourself. Never give up and always find that inner strength.*

Set Goals

Set goals and make it a point to achieve them, no matter what obstacles are put in your path. The goals that I set for myself as a teenager were to graduate from high school. I did that!

Get out of Ohio and away from all of those who tormented me. I did that one too!

I always wanted to go to college, but, never dreamt, in my wildest dreams that I could achieve that goal. I am currently doing that!

Never give up and always take control of your life. I may have had low self-esteem and thought of myself as ugly while growing up, but, I always made it a special point to take care of my hair and myself. I always felt that even though my hair was red and others bullied and teased me about my hair, my hair was still a part of me. I needed to take care of it. I was not going to live around those people forever.

Achieve Your Goals

By no means am I a weak person. I am very resilient. Once I moved out of Ohio and put my past behind me, I developed the attitude that "I could do or be whatever I wanted, within means".

While taking my oldest daughter to her baton competition, I realized while watching the whole process of how the competitions were being performed, that "WOW! I could do this"

As the teams were coming onto the floor to do their routines, I again thought to myself "I can do what those teachers are doing, if not better and it doesn't take a degree to learn this stuff". I made flyers, and made arrangements with the school to commence teaching after school hours in the gymnasium. I had way too many girls show up so I asked my dear friend to assist me.

While driving through the small town where I had lived; something inspired me to stop. I saw four teenage girls sitting on the church steps smoking. There was something special about these girls, and, it was not the gang lifestyle they were portraying. I couldn't resist stopping in front of the church where they were sitting to offer them free lessons and positions on my pom and dance teams. I stopped and asked them if they would be interested and they all jumped at the idea.

Of course, there were stipulations. I made them understand that their reputations were a reflection on my teams. Therefore, in order to participate, they had to abide by the rules that I had set for all of them to follow. Absolutely, no smoking, maintain good grades, no more sitting on the church steps and obey curfews and rules set by their own parents.

We practiced with music; we had successful fundraisers to afford the uniforms and competition fees. And then we competed. I could see their gratification when performing. These girls made me feel proud knowing them. When the girls had their uniforms on, they felt they were no different than their rivals. This was a sense of achievement for them.

I don't know where these girls are at today, but, I feel confident that I gave them worthiness and I hope they are all leading good lives, because, these girls deserved to have someone take time out for them. I did just that!

Ten years, fifty trophies and five U.S. Grand National Championship trophies later, I had achieved one of my goals in life and was very proud of my accomplishment. I retired from teaching poms and dance. I had become burned out. All my routines were beginning to look the same. So, I got out while I was still on top.

I wanted people to remember my achievements rather than my failures. I wanted to teach and I did just that.

After years of working in a factory, I discovered a new talent. I was always creative and I wanted to reach and achieve a new goal. As I was putting together Easter baskets one year, I decided that I wanted to open up a gift basket business. I started the business in my basement.

After developing a client base, I decided to open up a shop in downtown Auburn, Indiana. After less than six months of being open. I sold my business to another gift basket entrepreneur who had just recently been given the boot out of a mall in Indianapolis and wanted to open up in Fort Wayne.

By buying my business out this left their business with less competition. I accomplished exactly what I set out to do. Start up a business and succeed. I did just that and I was happy with myself.

Effects of Psychological Abuse
From Being Bullied

For so many years growing up, I had always felt like an underachiever because of the harassment I received from being a Redhead. It was those feelings that I had back then, that made me want to accomplish all my dreams.

In a big way, I believe I was trying to prove to all those bullies that Nancy "The Redhead" was not going to give up. Sure I wanted to forget my past because of all the hurt, but, I also want to succeed in life and let my past be that driving force.

As much as I would like to; I can not forget what happened, but, I can go on with life and encourage others who are being bullied to not let the bullies win. In doing so; never, ever, stoop to their level.

Piece of Paradise

Living on a lake was another goal which I wanted to achieve. I prayed numerous times to God for this dream to come true. Just to be able to look out every morning and see all the beauty; was something to be desired.

I didn't care if I lived in a big fancy house or a trailer. I just knew that I wanted to wake up every morning and look out at the beauty of what a lake has from within and the serenity that is projected.

To see the reflection of the trees and watch as the sun shines down giving the water the look of a sparkling diamond is truly magnificent.

This is the view from our living room
window in the middle of the winter

This was also a dream that my husband had. Together, we sold our house in town and found our little piece of paradise on a small fishing lake called *Terry Lake* in Hamilton, Indiana. Our home is just that "Our Home". Nothing fancy...only simple and very pleasuring.

Never Let Go of Your Dreams and Goals

Our home is a simple home and we love it. Our kids, grandkids and family love to gather in the summer and play on the lake. Camping, volleyball and fishing are the simple pleasures in life that I now enjoy.

I had a dream of being a writer and with the creative personality that God blessed me with I knew that I wanted to achieve that feat. I had once thought about writing scripts for sitcoms and movies. All those thoughts always stayed on the back burner for one reason or another.

I would watch reality television such as Big Brother, Amazing Race and Survivor and I would have dreams of playing in those games. I am always up for a challenge. I still want to write and I still want the challenge of playing and winning one of those television reality shows. I know I have what it takes and I know I could win. I am writing now so at least I am accomplishing one of those goals that I have wanted to achieve. I may not be a pro at writing, but, I am doing something I feel compassion about doing; and that is to raise awareness on the lasting effects of bullying.

As for the challenge of making it on one of those television reality shows, I guess we will just have to wait and see. Where there's a will, there's a way.

My husband and I did make it through the first round of casting calls for Amazing Race. That was exciting! We had to go to the CBS building in Chicago for the second round of call-backs. I remember sitting in a waiting area with other couples from all over the middle and eastern sections of the United States. We were all excited and were talking to one another, which later we found out was a major NO, NO. Afterwards, one of the contestants pointed to a sign that said "Absolutely no talking between contestants" Woops!

We had all made a major mistake and I believe it cost each and every one of us a spot on the show. One by one the couples were called in for their taped interview. When it was our turn to go into the room, I remember looking down at the rickety brown couch that we had to sit on, and I thought "I wouldn't even have this thing in my home, this is CBS, and shouldn't this couch be nicer?"

My husband and I sat on the couch with bright lights shining in our face all the while we were being prompted on how to answer questions that the casting director was going to ask. I couldn't stop yakking my jaws. I took over the interview. Call it nerves, or exuberance. I just didn't give anyone the time of day to talk or ask questions.

We left that casting call back interview with mixed emotions. AND! We never received a call-back. Imagine that!

I'm not going to give up though. Some day I will travel around the world in the "Amazing Race" and be casted on a remote island and nearly starve to death in "Survivor" for a million dollars. Or better yet be stuck in a house with total strangers "Big Brother". *If it's meant to be than it will be.*

To Be Humble

In life, we have all wanted "something better" or had to have "the best" there was. I have learned that material things do make you happy TEMPORARILY.

I have had that "brand new stick built house on a full finished basement" and a "brand new car. But, as with everything in life; the newness wears off very quickly. Then you want more. That kind of satisfaction is short lived.

I realize now that the secret to achieving life's greatest fulfillment, is not about getting "something better" or "having the best". It's about being happy, humble and true to you.

My garage is full of material things that I could never part with for one reason or another. When I die and go to Heaven; I can not take all of those things with me, so, why keep then now? My goal to reach for cleaning out my garage is to get rid of all the material things I can not use.

The older I get the clearer I see things and, the happier I become.

Remembering 9/11/2001

On the morning of my birthday September 11, 2001, I was marveling at how beautiful it was outside. The sky was blue and the sun was shining.

Every morning I turn the television on to listen to the news. But, on this day I couldn't help but to just sit outside and breathe in the fresh morning air.

I sat outside taking in the beauty as my daughter was getting ready for school. I stepped inside, just for a moment to get another cup of tea, when I heard an interruption from the television.

I could not believe what was happening. First one plane and then another and so forth. My phone was ringing off the hook with my family and friends calling and crying.

Watching all of this unfold right before our very eyes was unbelievable. Our very nation was under attack.

My daughter begged me to not send her to school for fear that more bad things could happen and she did not want to be away from home.

She felt safer with me. But, in good conscious I needed to send her to school so that she could talk and be around friends to relate how this was going to affect all of us. I reassured her that I was going nowhere and that I would be here when she came home.

I called the school to check up on her and the officials felt it was unhealthy for the students to acknowledge the events that were unfolding. I gave those school officials my opinion and disapproval.

These students (at least most of them) knew that something terrible was happening and they needed to talk about it. I knew that I had made a mistake to send my daughter to school that day. What was done was done.

That afternoon I did a lot of crying. All of the events really sunk in and it hurt me to see so many people affected by these terrorists. How could these terrorists justify their actions and why would anyone want to take a life. Unbelievable!

That evening I went out to dinner for my birthday. The waitress came up and took my order and when I asked for the complimentary desert, she looked at me and said "oh congratulations…Ohhhh…I'm sorry" This is the kind of response that I received for my birthday for the next couple of years after 9/11. But, I am still alive and I have God to thank for that.

For the rest of my life I will forever have to share my birthday with the day that 4,000 Americans lost their lives because of terrorists.

Harassment
Just another Name for Bullying

Being bullied while growing up, played a huge role in how I would allow myself to be treated as a grown working woman.

I made it a point in my adult life to never allow other adults to bully or as we call it as adults "harass" others. I was employed by two different companies that turned a blind eye to harassment of their employees.

Sexual harassment and retaliation for reporting it is the worst. I knew that this sort of behavior was not to be tolerated. I also knew that changes within an organization could not happen if this sort of bad behavior was not reported.

Many women actually feel that they must live with this form of harassment, for fear of reporting it would cause them to be dismissed or fired from their job. Termination from reporting abuse is REAL and it's against the law.

For me, I had already been tormented, bullied, and teased as a child and teen and I vowed to not let this happen again. Having to relive this as an adult was not going to be tolerated by ME. I was no longer a child and I had no reason to FEAR retribution for reporting this.

I was going to fight, and, if I lost my job in doing so, than so be it.

Well, I reported the harassment and I was retaliated against for doing so. I was terminated. Not quite one month after reporting the retaliation from reporting harassment, and violating my civil rights. I was terminated and I filed a lawsuit.

I did not care if I received one cent from this company. It wasn't about money! It was about standing up for what was right. I wanted to get the word out that this is serious.

Violating ones civil rights was not to be tolerated. By filing a complaint, and obtaining an attorney, I wanted this organization to take harassment seriously and change their policies with regard to employees civil rights.

If I could help even one person that was left behind in that organization, live a normal working life, free from harassment, than I would do just that.

I am a strong person and I will no longer sit on the sidelines. If someone is doing something wrong, I will stand up and I will not turn a blind eye. Having faith in God gives people the power to endure.

Faith
"Lost then Found"

However, there was one incident in my life where I can say without a doubt, that I had lost my faith. My daughter Amy was seven years old and my son James was only four when I found out that I was pregnant with my son Ross.

I decided that Ross would be that last child that I wanted to have. Three children were all that I believed I could handle.

On November 4, 1986 I was admitted into the hospital and was in labor for five hours. My son Ross was stillborn. Of course, I did not believe the doctors because I could have sworn that I heard him crying. The priest was called in and he was baptized. We had a small graveside service and for months afterwards my arms ached to hold him.

I thought I was being punished for something by God. What did I do so bad that God would take my son? WHY? I questioned my faith for two years.

In September of 1988 I found I that I was pregnant. This was the child that I would not have had, had Ross lived.

God knew this and for some reason he wanted me to know that I was not done bringing another soul into the world. My daughter Trisha was born April 28, 1989.

This whole thing made me think of how Jesus was sacrificed for our sins and what his mother went through to witness her son being murdered.

Ross died so that Trisha could be born. If Ross had lived Trisha most likely would not be here today. God knew this and he wanted me to know that he holds all the power.

Although, we may think that we have the power to make life changing decisions, God has the final say.

A very dear friend of mine, *Marti Suntken*, had also lost a son at birth. Each year the two of us find comfort in visiting our son's graves together. We visit on a date that is closest to when they both went to be with God in Heaven. This is the time of year that we both cherish very much, and, it is nice to share that moment of remembrance with someone who has experienced that type of loss.

Sharing and remembering is good for healing and I would highly recommend it to everyone. Make a day of it to visit lost loved ones and to always remember.

Sharing my Past

I never really discussed my past experiences with my children about the abuse that I suffered while in school. To bring the subject up was to relive it. To relive the past was too hurtful.

I was always aware while my children attended school for signs of abuse though. I was also ready at any given moment while they were young to step in if I had knowledge that some form of bullying was going on.

The whole subject has just been very tough to talk about for me in the past. Putting all of this down on paper seems to make me feel relieved and blessed. This was a long time coming.

Reflection

There is one thing that I have learned with the reflection of my past and that is that I have become a stronger person. I strongly believe in setting goals and achieving them.

Most everyone has experienced something negative or even traumatizing in their life by an event which may be for some, tragic. No matter what we may have gone through, find your faith and let that guide you to heal.

Never, ever, pity yourself. I'm sure some of you, who are reading this, may say that it is easier said than done. Make it a point in your life to heal and to get past whatever it is that is eating you up inside. No matter how much I was abused at the hands of others (bullies), I always tried my best to stay true to myself.

At times, it seemed impossible and yes! It is very hard to forget the bad experiences. Maybe, we shouldn't totally forget, after all, (in my case) the bullying molded me into the person I am today.

"It is because of the lack of compassion in children that I make it a point to show youth and my own children the importance of being compassionate to others". "It is because I was treated like a minority that I am not racist and I have taught my children the importance of treating all people of race and ethnicity as equals and to respect all people no matter". "It is because of the way the people treated me in church that I was determined to find a church where the congregation behaved as Christians and were true to the faith".

We all can change; sometimes it takes all that turmoil in life to lead us down that true path to God.

My pastor stated in a sermon one Sunday, the importance of surrounding yourself with fellow Christians. He also stated the importance of spreading the word of the gospel. If we can help just one person find their way to God it would be one more soul that reaches *Heavens* doors.

I believe that we need to turn all those negative feelings and memories into positive feelings. We need to find that wholesome goodness in ourselves. I will be the first to say that I am far from perfect and I have made my fair share of mistakes in life. With that being said; isn't it what life is all about? We live and we learn and that's what makes us all special human beings.

If I were to witness a bully in action today; I would stand up and intervene. I am not that child or teen that I was in school. I have persevered and I am strong.

Gods Gift

I truly believe that all of God's children are born with a gift. Most of us, if you are like me, haven't opened it up yet or are just beginning to unwrap it. Then again, like me, you have to discover the gift's whereabouts to reap its rewards. I am 48 years old and I have just discovered the gift that God gave me at birth and that gift is the "Gift to Reach Out" Through writing and compassion.

To find your gift, you have to first open your eyes. For those who are blind; open your minds. I turned a blind eye many times throughout my 48 years of life.

Have you ever felt throughout your life that everyone else was so lucky to have this and have that? So why can't I be that lucky.

I have recently discovered that it is not about luck, it's about reaching out and asking God through bold prayers and knowing when to open your arms to retrieve the gifts and rewards that are being given.

Some of us are given the gift of music, others are given the gift to build and construct. By searching deep from within, you may find that "God given gift"

If you are like me, you may keep on ignoring it until the time is right or until your old and gray and suffered many of life's hardships. Only, God knows when the time is right.

Of course, I wouldn't be writing this if God had not wanted me to go through all that life had to throw at me. With that being said, don't ever lose your faith.

See the beauty in everyone and everything *"we are all indeed special"*

Bullied Driven Advice

For those of you, who are being; cyber-bullied, **turn off the computer**.

For those of you, who are being bullied in school or a workplace, **report it**.

Never ever feel pity on yourself. *"Feeling pity upon oneself is truly a waste of energy"* Always stand tall and hold your head up high.

If someone calls you a name, just remember this saying (which goes back to my childhood days)

"Sticks and stones may break my bones but names will never hurt me"

Experiencing *negative* thoughts, think **positive**.

Most importantly…..Find your Faith

God truly loves each and every one of us AND he gave his only son Jesus Christ to save us from our sins.

Jesus Christ is our Savior

Always remember what Jesus went through before his death and think to yourself "is my suffering worse than the pain and sufferings that Jesus endured before his death?"

Rise above all others with care and compassion.

Every time you get the chance **"give to those in need"**.

If you feel that your life is in a rut, **"make a positive lifestyle change"**

The path to God and Our Lord Jesus Christ is an Amazing path to follow. Join fellow Christians on a walk that will lead us all to Heavens Doors. Find a Church and join the Congregation. Be a part of the bigger picture that lies ahead.

I was inspired to write my story by my husband Don Renner with the inspirational guidance of my faith

I want to dedicate this book to all of my children, my parents and to my family and friends and especially my husband **Don Renner**

My Parents: William and Karan Knapp and James Renner

My Children

Amy K, James, Lora, Ross, Trisha, Amy, Brian, Lori and Jason

My Grandchildren:

Gage, Ethan, Keegan, Spencer, Kyle, Max and the one in the oven

My Siblings

Kenny, Billy, Rich, Jim, John, Joe, Koog, Sis, MaryAnn, Therese, Maggie, Jane, Eve, Angie and Sheila

My Dear Friends:

Cheri, Laura, Brenda, Dawn, Ruth, Marti, Connie, Connie, Jerry, Judy, Melissa, Bridget, Amy

E-mail: n49renner@gmail.com

"We are all indeed special"

I reside in Hamilton, Indiana with my husband. We have a combined family of four daughters, three sons, six grandsons and another grandchild on the way (girl or boy?)

The lake in which we live on is a small fishing lake. Swimming, fishing, entertaining and cooking out for family and friends is what our summers are all about.

My husband and I attend the Pleasant lake Mennonite Church in Pleasant Lake, Indiana. The congregation of the church is our new extended family.

"We love life and we love one another"

CPSIA information can be obtained at www.ICGtesting.com
Printed in the USA
LVOW041547031111

253399LV00004B/105/P